365 QUOTES

FOR YOUR SUBCONSCIOUS MIND

YOUR SUBCONSCIOUS MIND - THE OBEDIENT SERVANT THAT TAKES YOU AT YOUR WORD

IRENE XANDERENA

ISBN: 979-8-8690-2957-7

Published by
Eyereneeswords
Email: life@eyereneeswords.com
Website: www.eyereneeswords.com

Contents

Introduction

Welcome to the world of "Whispers of Wisdom: Unleashing the Power of Quotes for the Subconscious Mind"–a collection of profound and thought-provoking quotes that will ignite the dormant potential within your subconscious.

In this enlightening book, I invite you to explore the transformative power of words and their ability to penetrate deep into the recesses of your mind, awakening new insights and perspectives. Each carefully curated quote acts as a catalyst, gently nudging your subconscious to expand its horizons, challenge limiting beliefs, and embrace positive change. Whether you seek inspiration, guidance, or a fresh perspective, these quotes serve as a window into the vast reservoir of wisdom that resides within you.

Get ready to be inspired, empowered, and forever transformed by the power of quotes. Quotes possess a unique ability to penetrate the layers of our conscious thinking, making a direct connection with the subconscious. They act as powerful messengers, gently whispering profound truths, insights, and inspirations into the depths of our being. These concise and carefully crafted words have the extraordinary power to stir emotions, challenge our perspectives, and ignite a spark of change within us.

The subconscious mind, with its boundless capacity for learning and processing information, is constantly absorbing and assimilating the messages it receives. Quotes, with their concise and impactful nature, effortlessly bypass the analytical mind and implant themselves deep within the subconscious. They have the potential to reprogram our beliefs, alter our thought patterns, and ultimately shape our reality.

So, join me on this captivating journey and explore the profound impact of quotes. Prepare to be inspired, enlightened, and empowered as you embrace the power of words to shape your inner world and manifest the positive changes that you desire.

Dedication

I dedicate this book to the mysterious force that dwells within us all – the subconscious mind. It is a testament to your power, your influence, and your ability to shape our thoughts, emotions, and actions.

I dedicate this book to the readers, the thinkers, the truth-seekers, and all those who seek to uncover limitless possibilities the subconscious mind holds within. May these quotes serve as stepping stones, illuminating the path towards a deeper understanding of your true selves. May they inspire you to embrace the beauty and complexity of your subconscious, and to harness its potential for growth and healing.

I dedicate this book to the philosophers, the psychologists, and the spiritual guides, whose wisdom and insights have paved the way for a deeper understanding of the subconscious mind. Your teachings have shed light on the intricacies and wonders of this vast realm, guiding us toward a greater awareness of our inner workings. Your contributions have been instrumental in shaping the content of this book.

To my loved ones, my pillars of support and inspiration. This book is dedicated to you, who have believed in me and my vision from the very beginning. Thank you for your encouragement, your love, and your understanding.

Acknowledgment

I am deeply grateful for the opportunity to express my appreciation and acknowledge the creation of this book of quotes dedicated to the subconscious mind.

This project has been a labor of love, and I am honored to have been able to contribute to the realms of self-discovery and personal growth. First and foremost, I would like to thank the subconscious mind itself, the wellspring of infinite possibilities and untapped potential within each of us. It is a profound force that guides, shapes and influences our lives in ways we may not always be aware of.

This book is a testament to the belief that by exploring and harnessing the power of our subconscious, we can unlock new levels of understanding and transformation. I am also indebted to the countless thinkers, philosophers, and visionaries who have shared their wisdom and insights on the subconscious mind. Their profound books have served as a beacon of inspiration, guiding me on this journey of exploration.

Moreover, I extend my heartfelt gratitude to the readers who will embark on this journey of self-discovery and self-awareness through the pages of this book. Your willingness to engage with the subconscious mind, to delve into the depths of your own psyche, is a testament to your commitment to personal growth. It is my sincerest hope that the quotes within these pages will resonate with you, ignite a sense of curiosity, and inspire transformative introspection.

I would like to acknowledge the support and encouragement of my loved ones, who have been a constant source of inspiration and belief in my abilities. Your unwavering support, feedback, and faith in my work have fueled my determination and commitment to this endeavor.

I am grateful to have had the privilege of creating this book of quotes for the subconscious mind. It is my sincerest hope that it serves as a catalyst for introspection, growth, and self-discovery for all those who engage with its pages. May it unlock the doors to our subconscious minds, revealing the profound wisdom and limitless potential that lies within us all.

Preface

Iwelcome you to a realm beyond the conscious mind, a dimension where thoughts, emotions, and desires intertwine in a symphony of untold potential. The subconscious mind, often elusive and enigmatic, holds the key to understanding our deepest selves. It is the gateway to our dreams, our fears, and our untapped potential.

Within its depths lie the answers to questions we may not even know to ask. It is here that our true desires and aspirations take root, waiting to be unearthed and nurtured. Inspired by the works of philosophers, psychologists, and spiritual guides, this collection of quotes seeks to unravel the mysteries of the subconscious and shed light on its profound influence on our lives.

I have carefully chosen each quote to provoke thought, ignite introspection, and stimulate the imagination. As you navigate through these pages, let your mind wander freely, embracing the power of the subconscious to guide your journey.

Allow the words to seep into your consciousness, awakening dormant thoughts and emotions. Engage with them, question them, and let them ignite a spark within you.

But be warned, dear reader, for the subconscious is a realm of both light and shadow. It is here that our deepest fears and insecurities reside, ready to challenge and provoke us. Yet, if we dare to face these shadows, we open ourselves to profound growth and transformation.

The purpose of the book is to inspire self-reflection, to encourage you to dive beneath the surface and confront the depths within. It is a testament to the infinite potential that lies within each one of us.

In this journey, you are not alone. Countless philosophers, psychologists, and spiritual thinkers have dedicated their lives to unraveling the mysteries of the subconscious mind. Their wisdom, their insights, and their profound understanding of the human psyche serve as invaluable companions on this quest for self-discovery. May this book of quotes serve as a guiding light, illuminating the path toward a deeper connection with your subconscious mind.

May it inspire you to explore the uncharted territories within, unlocking the hidden treasures that lie dormant. And may it empower you to embrace the fullness of who you are, as you embark on a transformative journey of self-realization. With an open heart and an inquisitive mind, let us embark on this exploration of the subconscious mind, where the possibilities are as limitless as the depths within.

Irene Xanderena
November 2023

365 Quotes for Your Subconscious Mind

1.

What I do is more valuable than what I know.

2.

I do not doubt the impact I have on others. My daily habits inspire many. I continue being that lighthouse.

3.

Gratitude is my superpower.
Appreciation is my lifestyle.

4.

I am never too old to go after
my vision until I tell myself I
am too old.

5.

I Imagine the best scenario in all situations, then I let the law of attraction go to work.

6.

Sometimes I just lean back and observe; not everything deserves a reaction.

7.

When I see the beauty in myself and others; my aura, my energy field becomes irresistible.

8.

The greatest puzzle is life! All I must do is connect the pieces to create the life I want.

9.

I do not get angry with someone who doesn't know any better. It is a waste of time. Whenever I catch myself in an argument, I slap the fly on my cheek.

10.

One thing about life is that there will always be something. So, instead of focusing on the issue, I focus on the lesson.

11.

The surest route to improve my skills is to put in the time.

12.

Sometimes life may feel like a gym membership with a very complicated cancellation policy. I get my money's worth and keep showing up!

13.

I make sure I get your annual average vaccine and stop the spread of "average!" I Rise above average.

14.

My health is my greatest resource.

15.

The difference between thought and action is decision. So I just get it done.

16.

Life is a process of learning, unlearning, and relearning. I am the teacher and the student.

17.

It is okay for me to get angry, but I don't remain in anger.

18.

Change is automatic, but progress is not. When I want to move from one level to the next, it is about progress and not change.

19.

I always keep my attitude in check. I know even when I am well dressed, nice clothes will never cover a bad attitude.

20.

Energy is everywhere, but not all energy is the same. I am selective with the energy I allow in my space.

21.

I can be sincere and work hard all my life, yet still end up broke and unhappy. Instead of being a good worker, I practice being a good listener.

22.

Many want to be successful and there is nothing wrong with that. As for me, I must first define what success means to me personally instead of using other people's definitions of success.

23.
Anything in life is a product of the meaning and value I give it.

24.
Even when I am right, I don't flaunt it! Being a good listener may be just what is needed.

25.

Sometimes I go after something not because I want it, but because my upbringing has programmed me to want it. Now I know better.

26.

There is nothing more therapeutic than action. I will take that first step.

27.
Those who can't see my vision will tell me it can never be done. I do not need their approval unless I don't believe in my own vision.

28.
I will not try to fit into Cinderella's shoes! It will not fit! It is not mine! I will put on my own shoes and create my own reality.

29.
Having a heart of gratitude is a lifestyle. Instead of seeing the cup as half full or half empty, let's start with the cup. I have a cup.

30.
I remain in chains when I care more about what others think of me than what I think of myself. What others think of me is none of my business.

31.

I can spot the toxic impulses around me. For one week I will keep a journal and do the three Cs! I will not complain, criticize, or compare.

32.

Clarity is a state of mind! Courage is a state of mind! Doubt is a state of mind! I have choices.

33.
He who has resources has choices. I keep learning, I keep creating, I keep adding value.

34.
When I have success, I am extra weary. When I am angry, I take no action.

35.
If I don't understand, I will ask! I need my communication to be clear.

36.
My opinion is my point of view, it does not necessarily make it true.

37.
*Ideas are things to play with.
If I hold on to them for too
long, they die.*

38.
*If I am not willing to downgrade
my lifestyle for a year or two, to
build the lifestyle that I want
in the future, this means I care
too much about what people
think of me.*

39.

I will never underestimate the power of my voice. My voice matters and I will use it!

40.

Seeing something is not the same as noticing it. Doing something is not the same as being present in the act.

41.
Motivation will get me going.
Speech will get me fired up. But
only discipline will give me the
strength to stay committed to
my vision.

42.
I am comfortable with being
uncomfortable. This pushes me
towards my goals.

43.
There is no greater satisfaction
than knowing my hard
work paid off.

44.
Ideas don't come out fully formed.
They only become clear when I
work on them.

45.

I never assume someone knows what I want from them. I make it a habit of telling people upfront what I want from them.

46.

I acquire stress when I take on a job I don't like to get money to pay for bills I have acquired.

47.

The process of changing any behavior starts with awareness. I cannot change what I am not aware of.

48.

I am okay with the fact that I am not for everyone.

49.

A seed will only grow when it is planted in something bigger than itself.

50.

Self-love is the balance between accepting myself as I am while knowing I deserve better and working towards it.

51.

I will never get back the life I wasted trying to be normal! I choose to be my authentic self.

52.

If I try, and I fail, it's time for congratulations. Most people wouldn't even try! I fail my way into success.

53.

My job is what they pay me to do. My work is what I was born to do. My job is my skill, my work is my gift.

54.

The fastest way to manifest what I want is to have a lifestyle of gratitude. These two words "thank you" will change my life.

55.

*I accept compliments but I don't
get attached to compliments.
I enjoy the moment and
then move on.*

56.

*Sometimes I must go through
life with blindfolds. I do this by
blocking what others think of me.
I create a tunnel vision and focus
on my dreams.*

57.
*The greatest book I should read is
"ME" I must know myself.*

58.
*Belief leaves room for doubt, it is
uncertain. Knowing is explicit
and clear.*

59.
*Once I see myself as a placebo,
I can direct that pill in any
way I want.*

60.
*Once I start thinking there is only
one way to get something done, I
limit myself. There are infinite
possibilities.*

61.

As long as I am breathing, it's a fresh start. Every second is a new opportunity.

62.

When my education is based on earning instead of learning, I will remain unfulfilled.

63.

My limitations are enforced when I start or end with "I'm only human.

64.

I would rather have scrapes and scratches and live a limitless life than have no marks but live in a box.

65.
Having a goal without doing the work becomes an illusion.

66.
When my energy is going in different directions, I am sending out mixed vibrations. When I focus my energy; I focus my mind.

67.
I have learned to laugh at myself so when others laugh at me, well I did it first.

68.
I do not need to control how others view me. Instead, I control how I respond to how others view me.

69.

I am never going to be where I want to be because I am always going to be beyond where I currently am. So, I will relax and enjoy the process.

70.

Meditation is a tool that allows me to release thoughts that are active in my vibration.

71.
Avoid sabotage! I keep my ideas to myself until they are fully developed because not everyone will agree with me.

72.
I will stick to the plan! It's worth it.

73.

I embrace my weirdness. My source of power is whatever makes me weird, odd, strange, and different.

74.

In this world of endless distractions, if I want to achieve my goals, I have to prioritize and stay focused!

75.
*I cannot be a high achiever
if I don't feel good. I take care
of myself.*

76.
*When I believe in myself and I
continue being consistent with
my daily habits, the only outcome
is victory.*

77.

*My mental development does
not happen solely by what I read.
What I think about what I read is
of great importance.*

78.

*In some situations, it is good to be
nervous, it probably means I care.*

79.
Intentions are goals mixed with compassion. I aim to be intentional, conscious, and deliberate!

80.
I will be ready, but I will never be 100% ready. I will keep showing up!

81.

*I see with my eyes but I become
aware with my energy.*

82.

*I am intentional about anything
I put out in the universe. It's a
boomerang and comes right back.*

83.
When I get what I want and I am still not happy, I need to check my intentions.

84.
Many of my achievements have manifested through the path of obstacles along the way.

85.
Looking for a favorable outcome when I haven't done the work, is like expecting to get an "A" in a class I have not registered for.

86.
Sometimes I just let it flow with zero resistance.

87.

Just as a snake isn't a disabled lizard, but a unique reptile; I don't accept society's label of me. I accept myself as the unique human that I am.

88.

When I get to a point in my life where I do things for the joy, pleasure, and gratitude of it and not because I am trying to please others or any "God," I am free.

89.

When looking for friendship or a partner, first I ask myself "Will I date me?"

90.

Change doesn't always mean improvement, but without change, there can be no improvement.

91.

Life is like a buffet with lots of variety. But I don't load up my plate with what I don't want to eat.

92.

I have come to appreciate that the word "No" is not a negative word. It means I am assertive and know what I want or don't want.

93.
*When I choose to live with
no regrets, I take care of the
present moment.*

94.
*My beliefs shape my thoughts and
my thoughts govern my actions.*

95.
I pick up the paintbrush every morning and become the artist of my life.

96.
I did not come into this existence to live up to anyone's expectations.

97.

As a true wisdom seeker, I know how much I don't know so I keep expanding my knowledge.

98.

When I speak my truth, I run the risk of being offensive. Not everyone will agree with me and that's okay.

99.
I have made it a habit to invest in becoming the best version of myself.

100.
When I step into the lion's den, I have two choices: Get eaten or become a lion. No one can make that choice for me.

101.

When I have the energy, drive, and passion to do something today, I get it done. I may not have the same energy, drive, and passion tomorrow.

102.

Asking the right questions is the catalyst to knowing myself. When I want to know about myself, I ask myself the 3 Ws! What story am I telling? Why do I feel this way? When do I want to start?

103.
Someone feels better today because I exist, and I share my knowledge.

104.
To be creative, I must be able to express myself. If I am afraid to express myself, I cannot be creative.

105.
When I only focus on the destination, I lose the joy and passion of the journey.

106.
I know that sometimes the answer is not to step out of my comfort zone, instead all I need to do is expand my comfort zone.

107.
I remain grateful for those I can connect with on a mental level.

108.
I remain at ease not because everything is good, but because I see the good in everything.

109.

I will not limit myself by creating a problem for every solution.

110.

The better my attitude, the better I can overcome stressful situations.

111.

Sometimes, I must become a stripper! I strip off people's expectations of me, then I clothe myself in my own image and live up to my expectations.

112.

I must always be myself and not what society dictates! Society cannot put a label on me.

113.

It's a great thing to have support, but it's even greater when I believe in myself.

114.

I pick my words carefully and with kindness. Uttered words can be forgiven but not forgotten.

115.

I must love myself more so I can give love to others.

116.

I have learned to travel light. I enjoy the journey and let go of attachments.

117.

The beliefs I hold of myself form and shape the story that I call my reality. So, I always think of the best outcome for myself.

118.

I make plans, I am excited about my plans, and I know I must take action or there will be no outcome.

119.

When someone says negative words to me, first I observe and examine. If the words are true, I adjust. If the words are false, I smile, shake it off and keep moving.

120.

Another person's opinion of me is none of my business. I know my strengths and weaknesses. I know my value.

121.

As I propel people into becoming the best version of themselves, I do so for myself too.

122.

When I get hurt I don't remain there. I do not pretend that I'm not hurt. Instead, I feel the hurt and grow from it.

123.

The person who hurt me cannot heal me. I heal myself through the process of focusing only on gratitude and appreciation.

124.

Smiling is my shield. It is the way I set up my energetic boundaries and bounce any unwanted energy out of my energy space. I know the way I feel is the energy I will attract.

125.

People will always have an opinion about me. But I'm careful and I do not allow anyone who has not been in my shoes give me instructions on how to tie my shoelaces.

126.

Walking is a good metaphor for life. We rise and fall with each step. In life, I will have ups and downs, but I will keep going.

127.
I will not live an ordinary life to make others happy. I do not feel guilty about being extraordinary. What others think of me is none of my business.

128.
Feelings are okay, but if my feelings make me unhappy or make me feel like a victim, I take a break and find new feelings.

129.
Whatever I want from others, I must be it first! If I want respect, I start by respecting myself first.

130.
When I know of something that can benefit others, I share, I do not hoard.

131.
Happiness is not a destination.
Happiness is a process, a journey;
an intentional inside job.

132.
I start my day with appreciation
and gratitude. This is the
magic wand I use to drive away
unwanted vibes.

133.

I am the only person who sees life through my own eyes. So, when people think they know me, they only know what I choose to show them.

134.

When I start feeling sorry for myself; when I feel stuck and need direction, I practice random acts of kindness, and then beautiful things manifest.

135.
I am confident, I am bold, and I set healthy energetic boundaries.

136.
There is nothing new under the sun. So sometimes instead of trying to recreate the wheel, I just make the wheel better.

137.
Becoming the greatest version of myself is a lifestyle and not a goal. The habits I have today will show up in my life tomorrow.

138.
I am the energy I attract so, I protect my energy space.

139.
I regularly check to see how I feel about myself when I am by myself with no distractions.

140.
I can never be an authentic copycat. There is no point in trying to be someone else.

141.
I know the law of exchange is always active. I create more than I consume. I am a creator and not a spectator of my life.

142.
I don't chase. As a creator, I know my tribe will find me.

143.
My perception of myself can alter and change my DNA. I know about Epigenetics.

144.
There are no stars or Browne points to be won, so I don't waste my life trying to live up to other people's expectations.

145.
My thoughts are like seeds, once planted, they will grow. Weeds will come as negative thoughts to choke my vision. I uproot all weeds quickly and give them no attention.

146.
I never doubt my ability for I know that every day there is someone doing something that has never been done before.

147.
Responsibility is a discipline that I need to grow. When I avoid responsibility, I lack discipline and I will not grow. I am not afraid of responsibility.

148.
The universe cannot be deceived. What I wish for others is what I wish for myself.

149.
When people tell me that I am full of myself, my response is "If I am not full of myself, who should I be full of?"

150.
Whenever I am bothered by other people's opinions, I first admit to myself that I am bothered, and then I ask myself why it bothers me.

151.

When I keep saying yes, when I really mean "no" I disrespect myself and mislead others.

152.

I am not a prototype! There is only one version of me. No AI can replace me. So, I eat right, exercise, and take care of myself.

153.
It is okay to remove from my surroundings things that don't bring me peace.

154.
Health is holistic. It's not just about diet and exercise. I also channel my thoughts for healthy outcomes.

155.
It is a conscious choice to take 100% responsibility for my life.

156.
When I love what I do, I no longer count the hours, instead, I focus on my vision.

157.

*Social media is a tool to be used.
I am a user of that tool. I use the
tool; the tool does not use me.*

158.

*I don't attract what I want by
reading 100s of self-help books. I
attract what I want through my
daily habits.*

159.
Today, right now is the time to lay the foundation for what I want to do. I will not put it off.

160.
Happiness is self-generated. It is not something that another person can give me.

161.

Practicing appreciation and gratitude keeps me in alignment with my true self. When I am in alignment, negative energy becomes invincible.

162.

When I am about to move from one level to another, when my energy is shifting in the direction I want, I become aware! This is anticipation and not fear, so I welcome it.

163.

My negative emotions are indicators to let me know I am out of alignment with my true self. When they come, I recognize them, I am aware of them, but I do not remain in them.

164.

I know I can control the direction of my thoughts. I do this through my senses and that includes the people I interact with, what I read, what I watch, and what I give my attention to.

165.
*The solution I seek in any
situation begins when I change
my mindset.*

166.
*I am a vibrational Match
to everything I have ever
experienced before it manifested.
I pay close attention to how I
think and feel.*

167.
My home is within me and goes everywhere with me. I make sure I feel at home "at home."

168.
My past cannot be undone, nor can it be deactivated. But, my future is waiting to be created.

169.
It is good to work. But I will not work to a point where I can no longer have the life that I'm working for.

170.
I spend money to buy time. I do not sell my time to make money. My time is valuable, and it is my life.

171.

My life is the most important game I will ever participate in. I make it blissful.

172.

I am selective with my thoughts because I know every thought creates a scientific reaction. Thoughts create chemicals in my body.

173.
I am very careful with what I call myself. Labels are limitations.

174.
I am my greatest fan I am my best audience.

175.

I know who I am and have no desire to prove myself.

176.

My thoughts are like children. I don't judge my thoughts. I am a gentle observer of my thoughts.

177.
The greatest gift I can ever give the world is my personal experience.

178.
To be confident, I have to trust myself.

179.

When I start seeing other people as a reflection of myself, judgment disappears, and appreciation appears.

180.

I am at a point where I can hear other people's words, but their words no longer have an impact on how I live my life.

181.
The fastest way to love myself is
when I no longer compare myself
to other people.

182.
I take care of myself and my needs
because I take myself with me
wherever I go.

183.
I never let people who have never lived teach me how to live.

184.
Fear is the most accessible frequency. But I don't vibrate on that frequency.

185.
Being confident is not about being arrogant. It simply means I'm better than my last version.

186.
Understanding is great. Being understood is greater, but the greatest is being okay even when others don't understand me.

187.
*I did not come into this existence
to set others straight! It is not my
job. I came here for my own unique
experience.*

188.
True friendship is a gift.

189.
When someone has an issue with me but chooses not to discuss it with me, I know it is not my issue but theirs.

190.
No matter how hard I try, I can never read your thoughts. But what I can do is respond to you the way I would like you to respond to me. In love and kindness.

191.
Facing the reality I have been living will contradict the reality I want to create. I did not come into this existence to face reality. I came into this existence to create my own reality.

192.
My mindset keeps changing because every new destination requires a new mindset.

193.

I only have one body to last my entire lifetime so I take very good care of it.

194.

My body is like a computer and my thoughts are like the software. If I don't upgrade, I will keep hitting problems along the way.

195.
I do not internalize the way someone treats me. The way someone treats me says a lot about them.

196.
I know where I am going, and I will get there.

197.

I remain faithful to my vision, not from a place of anxiety and desperation, but from a place of knowing that it has already happened.

198.

When I use my GPS, I get step-by-step instructions. If I am given all the instructions at once, I may become overwhelmed. It's the same with my goals, I take them step by step.

199.
I do not suppress my feelings because I know suppressed feelings can build up toxins in my body. I express my feelings and grow from them.

200.
Not all stories are true. Not all history is true. The winners write stories that favor them.

201.
Forgiveness is an emotion. Pain is an emotion. When I genuinely forgive someone, I take my attention off the pain and replace it with another emotion.

202.
I remain authentic and flexible. I know how to bend without being bent, move without being moved, and change without being changed.

203.

When I care too much about what others think of me, they will be my master and I will be their prisoner.

204.

Spirituality is who I am as a human being. It is not a race, culture, religion, or practice.

205.
I will keep doing whatever brings me peace, joy, and happiness.

206.
Those who steal my time with energy-draining and time-wasting issues are guilty of an ethical violation of my time.

207.

Kind thoughts are good, and ethical thoughts are great! But without the corresponding action, they become mere entertainment.

208.

The healing process like an onion happens one layer at a time.

209.
I am very careful how I respond to flattery. For I know flattery usually precedes manipulation.

210.
I let my day be governed by the present moment. I put aside doubt, fear, assumptions, and limitations.

211.

*I know who I am, and I trust myself.
I do not seek external validation.*

212.

*I create joyful memories today so
when tomorrow's illusion becomes
today, there is stored-up gratitude
that overflows.*

213.
Instead of dwelling on those who let me down, I reminisce on those who hold me up.

214.
Life is not about waiting for things to get better. Life is about being joyful right now.

215.

I value my peace and my time. I do not waste either trying to expose another. That's the job of the universe, not mine!

216.

I appreciate those who can invoke both affection and anger in me. They are the ones that remind me of who I am.

217.
Although I live in the same world as billions of people. No matter how much we share, the same air, environment, food, etc. I always return to my own mental world.

218.
The world, through social media and other platforms, will keep trying to make me someone else. Remaining my authentic self is one of my greatest achievements.

219.
I am perfectly okay with being a work in progress and a masterpiece.

220.
Energy is contagious. I am highly selective about the energy I allow in my space.

221.

My body is a beautiful temple of love. Each cell, bone, organ, and muscle reacts to the love I send and the result is radiant health.

222.

I will never talk myself out of something I want just because I have not figured out a way to get it.

223.

Sometimes there is a gap between my desire and its manifestation. I don't get frustrated instead, I get to a place of knowing.

224.

I know I am responsible for my happiness and inner peace. But I still appreciate all who add to it.

225.

I can only be to others what I am first to myself. The way I see myself reflects what I give.

226.

I will not waste my time trying to get someone to see what they are not ready to see. It is not my job.

227.

My life is measured by the variety and content of my experiences.

228.

I do not appreciate people silently. I show my appreciation through words, action, and gratitude.

229.

My imagination is the gateway to my creativity. I use it well.

230.

Whatever I believe of myself today will show up in my future. I always think of myself from a position of strength.

231.
Everything I see in this world was only first an imagination. I see endless possibilities.

232.
I have goals, I have a vision and I know where I am going.

233.
*I discard who I have been
and embrace who I am now. I
keep evolving.*

234.
*I can only receive what I see
myself receiving. I never doubt the
possibilities.*

235.

When I take an action, I check to see the emotions behind it. I want to know if I am acting out of faith or fear.

236.

I align with the energy that I want. When I ask for success, I prepare for success and not failure.

237.
I engage in goodwill towards all. This is my superpower.

238.
I am patient and I will never do today what my intuition tells me to do tomorrow. My intuition is my guide.

239.
I have made it a habit to use my words to heal, bless, and prosper.

240.
To be successful I never force anything. I let it flow.

241.

*I know that storms come and go.
Life continues and the sun will
rise tomorrow.*

242.

*My expectations match my
desires. When I desire something,
I expect it.*

243.
My money works for me and not
the other way around.

244.
Doing what others want me to
do is work. Doing what I want to
do is play.

245.
Even my common sense is organized.

246.
Worrying is a waste of time and does no good. I will not entertain worry.

247.
I go where my talent is celebrated and appreciated.

248.
I have thoughts of harmony with myself, so my success is imminent.

249.
The more I know, the more responsibility I have.

250.
If I claim to know something yet I can't explain it, then I do not know it. Explaining something I know should come naturally.

251.

I do not go digging up my past. My life is now as I move into my future.

252.

I don't need to be different to be successful. All I need to do is practice what most people don't! I need to be consistent.

253.
Change is usually resisted and
met with opposition! I do not resist
change. I examine it.

254.
I know that every element of
rushing is laced with some form of
fear. I do not rush.

255.
I love to give, and I also never forget to take care of myself.

256.
I only become old when my mind gives its consent.

257.

*Even when I am on the right track,
I don't just sit there! I remain
in motion.*

258.

*I do not cling to what I have. I let
go and make room for what I want.*

259.

I continue to celebrate every obstacle conquered and every victory gained. Celebration strengthens my faith.

260.

The energy I radiate will attract the energy I desire. I remain intentional, authentic, and purposeful.

261.
*My entire life is based on the
quality of my thoughts.*

262.
*I am a creator and not a creature.
I am very selective in my thoughts.*

263.
Sometimes I will disappoint others. But I make sure I don't disappoint myself.

264.
I organize my thoughts to get the results I desire. It's like sending an email. I organize the letters of the alphabet to form words.

265.
*I never put anything in writing
that the world will not have access
to someday.*

266.
*When someone is trying to
intentionally annoy me, I don't
play their game. I leave the
playground and bring them
into my world.*

267.
When accused of arguing, I
respond with "No! I'm
expressing myself."

268.
I take responsibility for
my actions and accept the
consequences that come
with them.

269.
I do not compare myself to others.
I focus on my own progress
and growth.

270.
I hear other people's words and I
notice the smiles. But the loudest
language I observe is what they
do and what they show me.

271.

Sleep is like a magic potion that turns me into a functioning human being.

272.

I refuse to entertain PLOM–Poor Little Old Me.

273.
I choose faith over hope. Faith comes from a place of knowing while hope comes from a place of wishing. Faith is Laced with trust, while hope is laced with doubt.

274.
I welcome inspiration. It is the fuel that ignites the fire within me, propelling me towards great things.

275.
The laws of nature remind me that there are endless possibilities.

276.
The universe will provide my food but will not cook my dinner. Without some form of action, I will starve.

277.
Inspiration is like sneezing. I am never sure when it will come. But then "BOOM" just like that I get it.

278.
I am selective with my thoughts the same way I am selective when I go to a buffet. I only pick and choose what I want.

279.
I take no pleasure in doing things that incite anxiety. It makes no sense to be allergic to something and yet keep taking it.

280.
I do not subscribe to FOMO—Fear of Missing Out! I know as one door shuts another one opens.

281.
The best 10-letter word I know is "discipline." It turns dreams into reality.

282.
I live my life now. I know time does not repeat but keeps ticking.

283.
This is my life. No one can live it for me.

284.
I make it a habit to put in my absolute best all the time.

285.
When life throws a punch at me, I don't get bitter, angry, or resentful. I focus and recalibrate.

286.
It is perfectly okay to outgrow tradition. When I know better, I do better.

287.
I love giving but I am not responsible for those who are not ready to receive. While I see abundance, they see scarcity.

288.
I do not entertain suggestions or careless words from other people that do not define me. I simply hit the memory delete button.

289.
My habit is to express what inspires, elevates, heals, and blesses me.

290.
In this universe, I know that what I seek is also seeking me.

291.

I do not entertain unwanted thoughts. Thoughts manifest through emotions, so I keep my emotions in check.

292.

I look within to get validation. Looking for external things to validate me is the surest road to stress.

293.

I am only responsible for my reaction and I take no stake in the reaction of others in any situation.

294.

Life is a game. As I learn the rules of the game, I am filled with peace.

295.
My successes and lessons (not failures) required great courage and for that I am grateful.

296.
No one can push, inspire, or motivate me! It is 100% my responsibility.

297.

To get the result I desire, the energy and direction of my struggle matter and not the struggle itself.

298.

I am the thinker of my thoughts. Since no one breathes for me, no one thinks for me.

299.
I win not because I have the right credentials, but because I think I can.

300.
My thoughts matter. They are the energy and magnet that create my reality which shows up as my outcome.

301.
I only concentrate on the things I want and not on the things I don't want.

302.
I have learned the skill of visualizing abundance.

303.

When I have a thought that I want, I nurture it through my actions. It's like planting a seed. When I plant a seed, I don't dig it up every day to see if it is growing. Instead, I nurture it and I know that in due time it will grow. In due time, my thoughts will manifest.

304.

When I am driven by my ambition, it is a blessing. I go after what I want.

305.
I know that I have to parent and push myself. No one is going to do it for me.

306.
I place zero limits on my capacity to achieve my goals. I believe it so I can achieve it.

307.
It's no secret that what I am and what I become ultimately depends on what and how I think.

308.
I have been gifted with millions of mental workers. They are my brain cells and I use them and remain unstoppable.

309.
I remain stuck in a job or even in a relationship that no longer serves me when I choose to believe something that isn't true.

310.
People only change when they desire to change, not because I tell them to. I no longer repeat myself.

311.
I can control the direction of my thoughts.

312.
My expectation is anything I want it to be. My expectation is my desire and belief united in the same place.

313.
My dream, my vision, and my mission were given to me and not to them. I don't need them to validate me.

314.
Because I planned for my success, I knew it was inevitable.

315.

I stop explaining myself when I realize people only understand from their level of perception.

316.

The process of changing any behavior starts with awareness. I cannot change what I am not aware of.

317.
The greatest investment I will ever
have is myself.

318.
I don't need any more
confirmations to validate what I
already know.

319.

Once I refuse to give false beliefs and habits any attention, they die.

320.

I admit my bad habits so I can change them.

321.
I choose to be a flexible leader instead of a boss.

322.
Every day, I am given eighty-six thousand four hundred seconds. I cannot save any of this time, so I use it well.

323.

Self-neglect is when I don't maintain my inner peace at the cost of maintaining external peace.

324.

I always seek knowledge and wisdom to better understand myself and the world around me.

325.
Material possessions do not bring me lasting happiness and fulfillment. My happiness and fulfillment come from within me.

326.
I focus on my thoughts for I can control them through observation or selection.

327.

I am honest with myself and with others even when it is difficult.

328.

I remain prepared so when that opportunity comes, I am already in the receptive mode.

329.
*I do not suffer in my imagination
for I focus on only things
that I want.*

330.
*I don't waste my time arguing
about good and bad. I choose
to treat others as I would like to
be treated.*

331.

When others think I am foolish or stupid, it is none of my business because I am content with being myself.

332.

I have no enemies! I know that declaring someone my enemy means giving them my power. I retain my power because I do not entertain the thought of enemies.

333.
Living in the present moment is the key to true happiness. I refuse to speak ill of others for it only reflects poorly on me.

334.
I check my emotions; I refrain from anger for it clouds my judgment and leads to regrettable actions.

335.
Fear is only a result of my own perceptions.

336.
I must invest in my dreams because if I don't invest in my dreams, there will not be a harvest.

337.

I cannot schedule intuition and I cannot schedule inspiration, what I can do is remain in the receptive mode, so I receive them.

338.

I am a co-creator with the universe.

339.
My desires bring me joy. They do not torture me.

340.
My strength is displayed when I let go of attachments.

341.
I breathe now. My breath is not for yesterday, and I do not store up my breath for tomorrow.

342.
I am secure in who I am. It does not make a difference if you think I am right or wrong.

343.
A lack of gratitude blinds me
from observing the abundance
I have been given, and a
heart of appreciation makes
everything enough.

344.
Because I see myself as a part
of everything, I am a part of
everything.

345.
*Being what I want to become
is more effective than
talking about it.*

346.
*My gratitude list is the antidote
to any external factor intended to
provoke me to anger.*

347.

*I do not suffer from status anxiety
because I am not my credentials.*

348.

*Creating my reality is about
knowing what I want and then
connecting to things that will
make it work.*

349.
Focusing on something means not being anxious about it. Focusing puts me in the creative mode while anxiety puts me in the panic mode.

350.
I am a vibrational being. Getting into an argument will send a signal to the universe that I want more things to argue about.

351.
I use gratitude and appreciation to channel my focus to the things that I want.

352.
As I empower others, others empower me.

353.
*The universe gives me great ideas
and they are mine to create.*

354.
*I show love when I choose to
get involved.*

355.
*My acts of kindness, big or small,
make a difference.*

356.
*I feed areas of my life with a
lifestyle that enhances growth.*

357.
When I am around people
and places, I pay attention to
how I feel.

358.
When something is in the past, I
leave it alone.

359.
When my emotions are high, I do not trust my thoughts, I do not make quick decisions.

360.
Today I build my legacy by creating footprints for others to follow.

361.
With a mindset of love, positive energy flows.

362.
I am not arrogant but I know everything starts with me.

363.
My mind is conditioned to only
see gratitude, appreciation,
and lessons.

364.
I deal with my doubts before
I share my vision with myself
or anyone.

365.
I choose clarity.

Bibliography

1. **"Blink:** The Power of Thinking Without Thinking" by Malcolm Gladwell: While not solely focused on the subconscious mind, this book explores the concept of rapid, intuitive decision-making. Gladwell delves into the role of the subconscious mind in our snap judgments and highlights its impact on our overall decision-making process.

2. **"Man and His Symbols" by Carl Jung:** In this insightful book, Jung explores the symbols and archetypes that populate our dreams and collective unconscious. It offers a comprehensive understanding of the subconscious mind and how it influences our thoughts, emotions, and behaviors.

3. **"Subliminal:** How Your Unconscious Mind Rules Your Behavior" by Leonard Mlodinow: Mlodinow delves into the realm of the subconscious mind, uncovering its immense power in shaping our behavior and decision-making processes. Through engaging anecdotes and scientific research, he reveals the subtle ways our unconscious mind influences our daily lives.

4. **"The Biology of Belief:** Unleashing the Power of Consciousness, Matter & Miracles" by Bruce H. Lipton: Lipton's book explores the connection between the mind and the body, emphasizing the role of beliefs in shaping our reality. He delves into the subconscious mind, discussing

how our thoughts and beliefs influence our biology and overall well-being.

5. **"The Hidden Messages in Water" by Masaru Emoto:** Emoto's book explores the idea that our thoughts and emotions can affect the molecular structure of water. Through a series of captivating experiments, he suggests that our subconscious beliefs and intentions can have a profound impact on our physical and emotional well-being.

6. **"The Interpretation of Dreams" by Sigmund Freud:** Considered one of Freud's most influential works, this book delves into the realm of dreams and their significance in understanding the subconscious mind. Freud's psychoanalytic approach provides a fascinating exploration of the hidden meanings and desires that reside within our dreams.

7. **"The Mind Illuminated:** A Complete Meditation Guide Integrating Buddhist Wisdom and Brain Science" by Culadasa (John Yates): While primarily a guide to meditation, this book provides a deep understanding of how the mind works, including the role of the subconscious. It offers practical techniques to develop mindfulness and insight, leading to a greater understanding and mastery of the subconscious mind.

8. **"The Power of Your Subconscious Mind" by Joseph Murphy:** This classic book explores the power of the subconscious mind and how it can shape our lives. It offers practical techniques and insights to harness the

subconscious and unlock its potential for personal growth and success.

9. **"The Seat of the Soul" by Gary Zukav:** This book delves into the spiritual aspects of the subconscious mind. Zukav explores concepts such as intuition, intention, and soul evolution, offering insights into how our subconscious influences our spiritual growth and connection to the world around us.

10. **"Thinking, Fast and Slow" by Daniel Kahneman:** While not exclusively about the subconscious mind, this book delves into the dual systems of thinking: the intuitive and automatic subconscious, and the reflective and deliberate conscious mind. It offers a comprehensive understanding of how these systems interact and influence our decision-making.